THE FOREX CHECKLIST

Why This Book Was Created

I started trading many years ago and I fell in love with the ability to make money fast.

However, I soon realized that I could lose money just as fast. I took a big loss a while back. Then another. And then many consecutive losses after that. I couldn't understand why my money-making system suddenly stopped working. So I took some time off to clear my mind.

I began reading and studying everything I could get my hands on. After spending much time tweaking my strategy, I finally found the issue.

It was leverage. That, and not sticking to my plan.

Leverage is a double-edged sword. It can drastically increase your position size, or it can drastically reduce your position size. It's all about being on the right side of volatility.

Regardless of what you are trading, price at times will reach certain levels. It can swing to the highest level in 50 days or it can drop to the lowest level of the decade. Certain scenarios will occur in which you can risk using higher leverage, such as when price overshoots to the downside or the upside. Alternately, there are situations where only lower leverage should only be allowed, such as when following the trend.

I noticed that when I traded with less leverage and used it more effectively, my trading improved.

But not completely.

If you are not careful, that feeling you get when you effortlessly make $1000 in minutes can give you a false sense of your ability. It's like a drug. And like a drug, many traders, myself included, continuously seek that same fast reward. Unfortunately, if you're not careful, that usually ends up in a loss.

Understanding this led me to the realization that the biggest flaw to my trading was me.

Focus is limited in the body and more useful if you know how to control it. Your body uses energy to focus and, like any muscle, your brain eats up a lot of energy during strenuous activities. This is why I like to get my most important things done first thing in the morning.

But there will always be times when you are under pressure or times when your focus meter is low, or both, which will lead to irrational behavior and irrational trading.

For instance, after making a nice profit, I would often put money right back to work again, sometimes too quickly, sometimes on a "hunch," and end up with a loss. Other times I would try to make up for a loss and end up with yet another loss. I had to figure out how to gain control of this system.

This is what led me to develop a checklist.

1. Find the direction of the trend.
2. Find out where price is now compared to past prices (is it at highest or lowest level, and why is it there?).
3. Locate a high-probability pattern (the longer the time period observed, the more reliable the chart will be).
4. Adjust leverage accordingly.
5. Do not trade under any other circumstances.

I created this book to be a simple tool that you can use during the course of your trading day. I hope this helps you as much as it has helped me.

Your Everyday Checklist

In this section:

1. Finding the Direction of the Trend

2. Understanding the Current Price Level

3. Locating a High-probability Pattern

4. Adjusting Leverage

5. Do Not Trade Under Any Other Circumstances

FORWARD
LEFT
RIGHT

Finding the Direction of the Trend

Trading in the direction of the overall trend is vital to making this system work. Prices usually tend to trend in a certain direction at a given time, either upwards, downwards, or sideways. And remember, for each time frame you observe there could be a different trend. For example, the daily chart could be in an uptrend, while the monthly chart could be in a downtrend.

The way we make money here is by riding the wave of the trend. It is important that you familiarize yourself with multiple time frames each time you sit down to trade.

At the beginning of every trading session I will first zoom out to the weekly or daily chart. This gives me the best understanding of where the price has been heading for the past few years.

In the picture above, you can see there are many different trends, with one large overall trend. You can easily see by looking at the 200 day moving average that this overall trend is pointing down.

Fundamentals that you read about are typically useless as the market has already discounted the price, and I call them "funny-mentals". I am primarily a trend trader with touches of hunches based on about twenty years of experience. In order of importance to me are: (1) the long term trend, (2) the current chart pattern, and (3) picking a good spot to buy or sell. Those are the three primary components of my trading. Way down in a very distant fourth place are my fundamental ideas and, quite likely, on balance, they have cost me money.

- Ed Seykota

Understanding the Current Price Level

Once you know the direction of the trend, the next step is to understand the current price. Is it near the 200-day high or maybe the 200-day low? What are the current factors behind the surge or the drop? What is the current sentiment?

A base strategy could be buying the currency of a country that has very favorable current economic conditions, while selling the currency of a country going through geological, political, banking, or other economic issues.

Having a good understanding of the country's economies will help your trading greatly. For example, there are certain currencies that will appreciate during a risk-on environment, such as the Australian dollar (AUD) and New Zealand dollar (NZD). Safe-haven currencies such as the Swiss franc (CHF) and the Japanese Yen (JPY) tend to appreciate during risk-off environments.

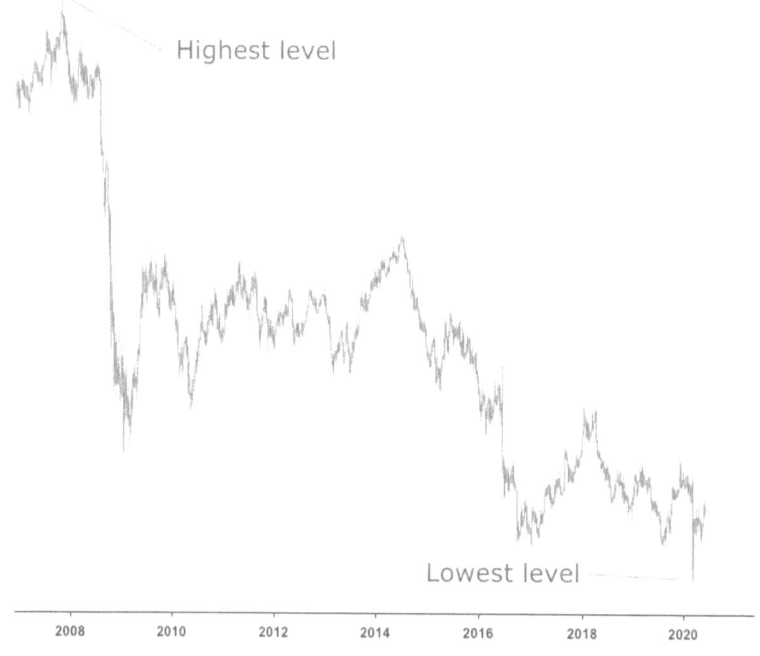

Volatility is greatest at turning points,
diminishing as a new trend becomes established.

- George Soros

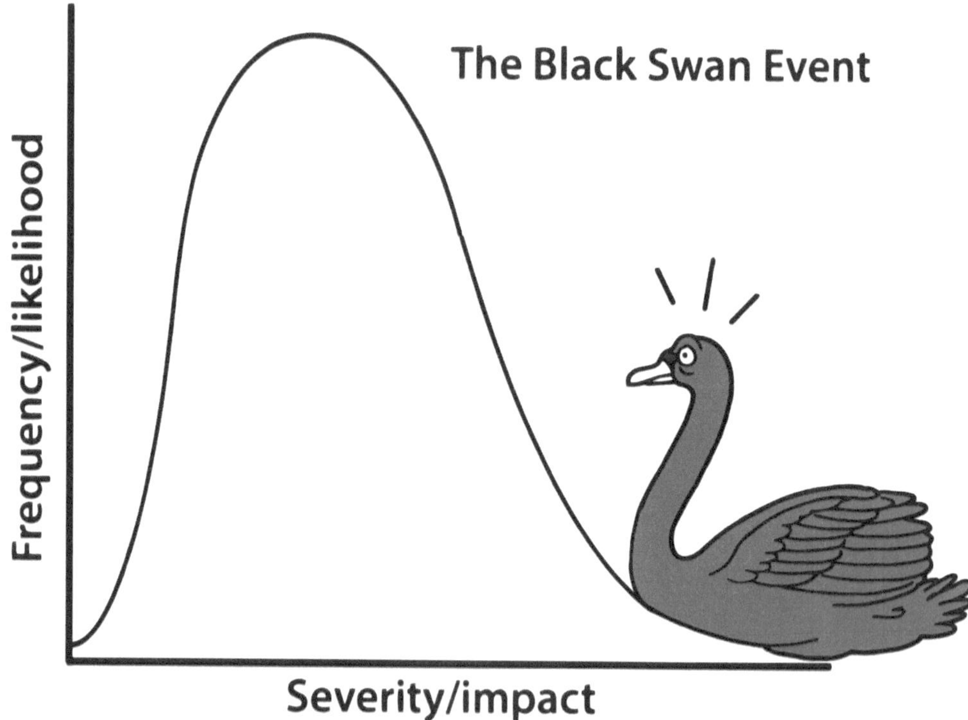

Frequency/likelihood
The Black Swan Event
Severity/impact

Locate a High-Probability Pattern

There are certain patterns that tend to follow a certain path most of the time. These patterns tend to be successful 65-70% of the time. Although assigning an exact probability is difficult, these patterns typically form due to the real-time demand for the currency, giving you an inside look as to whether the bulls or the bears are in control. Therefore, for the best chance of success, only place your orders on these patterns.

You must always use strict stop-loss and limit orders. This helps you jump out automatically if the pattern breaks, while helping you capture the full amount of the profit for the risk you took. I personally don't like to use anything less than a 3:1 profit/loss ratio. This means that for every trade I take, I aim to triple my return or take a loss of 1/3 of the trade placed. I like to aim for a 4:1 or a 5:1 ratio or more if possible.

Of course, you will have some losses here and there. But the point is to embrace them and learn from them and realize, if doing this correctly, over time, the law of large numbers will come into play and will put you ahead.

The trading patterns most likely to result in profit are:

Cup and Handle/Inverse Cup and Handle
Head and Shoulders/Inverse Head and Shoulders
Rising/Falling Wedges
Ascending/Descending Triangles
Double Top/Bottom
Triple Top/Bottom

Section II describes more fully what each of these looks like, as well as how to trade them.

Wide diversification is only required when investors
do not understand what they are doing.

– Warren Buffett

Adjust Leverage Accordingly

When it comes to using leverage, you must be extremely careful. Leverage can either work greatly in your favor or it can work greatly against you.

You won't always be able to pinpoint the perfect trade scenario, but you can get a better idea of the odds of a winning trade by learning high-probability patterns. My favorite patterns are described in step 3.

In the pic below, we have a triple top. It is one of my favorite chart patterns because of its reliability. If the resistance level is not breached, price will most likely come down and come down strong as sellers are gaining control. This is a scenario in which I would use an increased amount of leverage.

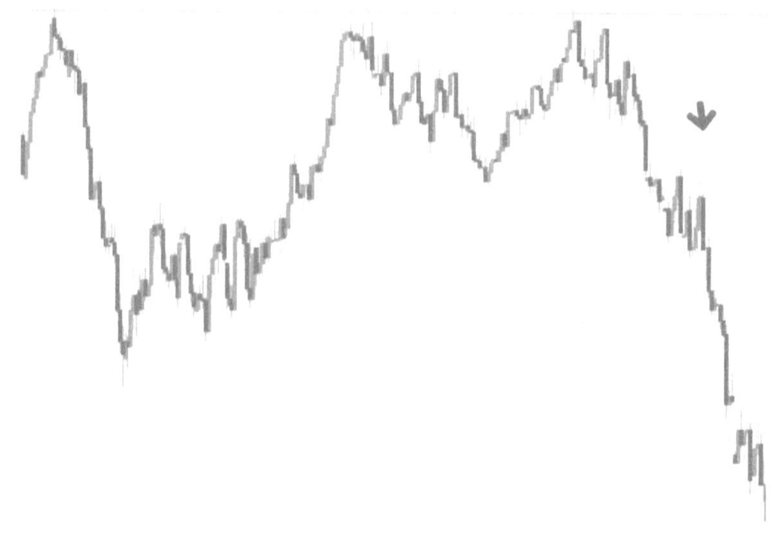

Something to keep in mind is the time frame of the pattern. Remember, use the weekly or daily chart to find the *direction* of the trend and use the 1- or 4-hour time frame to find your chart patterns to *trade*.

When trading a longer time frame, you never want to load the boat unless you are using a stop-loss. A stop-loss is a valuable tool that gets you out of your position at a set price if the trade does not go as planned. It is vital that you use stop orders or could be taken out, especially when trading longer time frames as they could tend to keep the trend going for longer than expected.

Be careful not to put your stop too close though, because as you see in the previous picture, price can whipsaw and take out your stop-loss if you put it too close.

I had a very humbling learning experience a while back, trading with high amounts of leverage. The pattern looked too good and the price went extremely low. I thought, "How could it go even lower?" But it did. By a lot.

This taught me to have an understanding of support and resistance levels so you can place your stop and limit orders effectively. The more leverage you are using, the tighter the stop should be. The less leverage you use, the more volatility you are able to endure.

Another thing to watch out for is how currencies' volatility can differ. One such example is the British pound (GBP). The pound, also known as the stirling, tends to make big moves up or down, so be sure to use very little leverage when just starting out in order to gain some experience.

Do NOT Trade Under Any Other Circumstances

After trading for many years, I have tried and failed many times. But I have also learned much from it. And while this is not the only "trade strategy" out there, it is one that I have developed over time through all of my trials and errors.

This guideline only works when you follow each step consistently. While using this method, do not stray from the plan.

In a nutshell, this strategy emphasizes placing trades on high-probability patterns. If the pattern fails to materialize, then you get out with a small loss. When the pattern does materialize, you ride the trend to the next support level at which you are comfortable, but by at least a 3:1 profit/loss ratio.

This means you should only place the trade if you are able to profit 3x what you would lose if the trade goes the other direction. For example, say you find a pattern in a downtrend that has found support. You then place your stop slightly past the support level, giving you enough space in case the price retests that region.

After, you are going to place your limit order slightly before the level of resistance you are looking to reach. This will give you a better chance of your order getting executed.

The law of large numbers, which is a fundamental concept in psychology, states that over time as the sample size grows, the average tends to lean toward the average of the entire sample. That's why it is important to let your pips run and let the pattern play out. If done correctly, this will allow you to make up for small losses, and over time, will put you ahead of the game.

The most important role of trading is to play great defense, not great offense. Every day I assume every position I have is wrong. I know where my stop risk points are going to be. I do that so I can define my maximum possible drawdown. Hopefully, I'll spend the rest of the day enjoying positions that are going in my direction. If they are going against me, then I have a game plan for getting out.

– Paul Tudor Jones

SOME HELPFUL TOOLS

In this section:

1. Candlesticks

2. Chart Patterns

3. Moving Averages

SELL
BUY

Candlesticks

In this section, I have put together a basic list of candlesticks for you to follow that will help give you an idea of where the price could be headed. Remember, the farther out the time frame of the chart, the more reliable it will be.

Hammer

- Bullish reversal candle
- Opposite of a shooting star
- Gets its name from its hammer shape, with a long wick followed by a small body

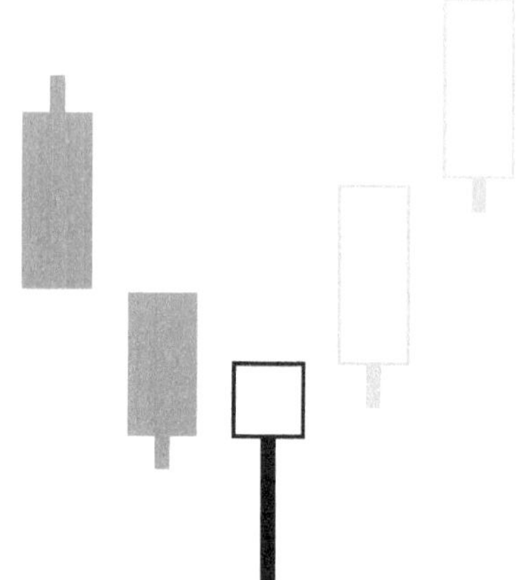

Inverted Hammer

- Bullish signal found at the bottom of a downtrend
- Reversal signal to the upside
- Gets its name from its hammer shape
- Small body, long upper wick, little or no bottom wick

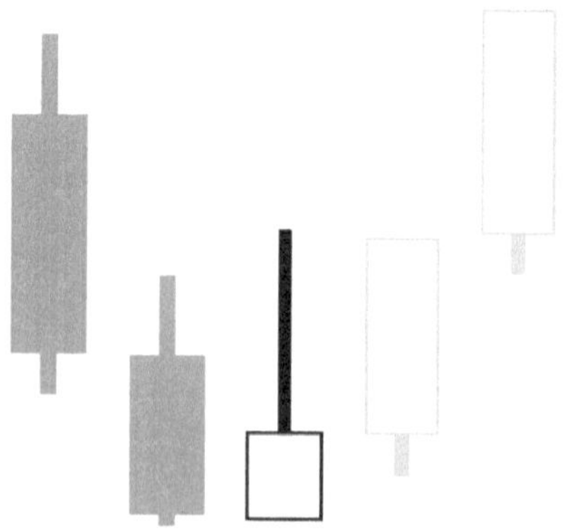

Dragonfly Doji

- Occurs during a downtrend
- Indicates buyers are becoming more dominant
- Occurs when sellers are able to push prices downwards, but support is found and pushes it back to the open

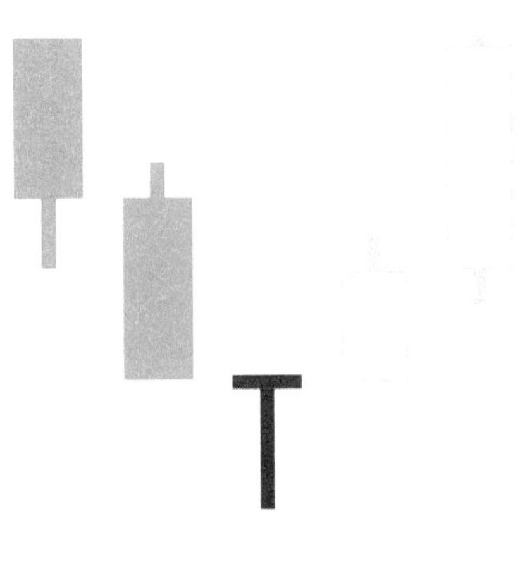

Bullish Engulfing

- Shows strong buying pressure
- Usually appears at the bottom of downtrend
- Opens at or below the previous candle's close
- Body then engulfs the previous candle and closes above its open

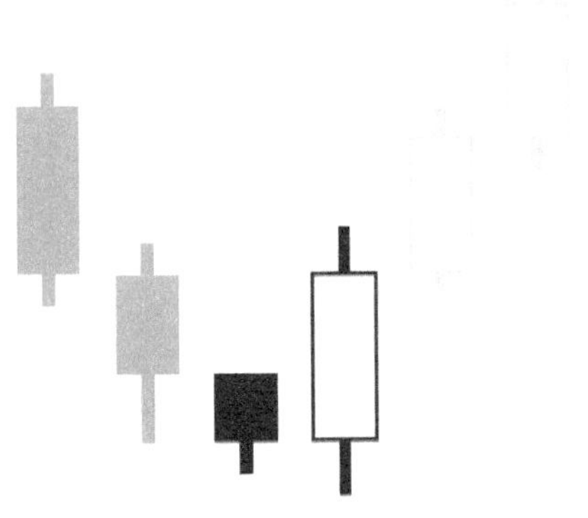

Piercing Line

- Demonstrates a high level of sellers, but buyers are gaining control
- Found at the bottom of a downtrend
- Tends to gap up at times due to high volatility

Morning Star

- Opposite of the Evening star
- Forms after a downtrend
- Indicates a reversal could be near
- Warns of weakness in a downtrend

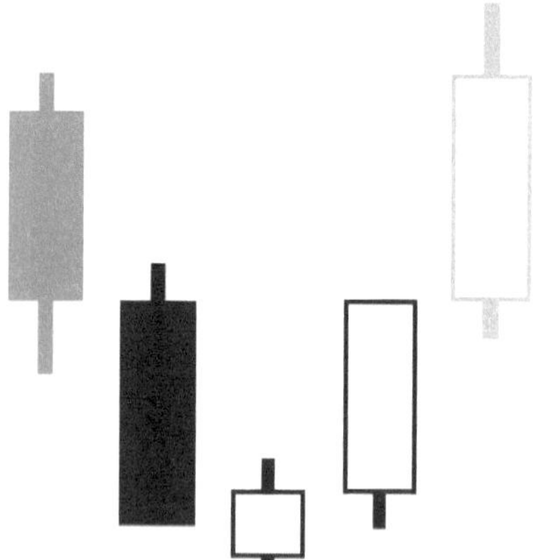

Shooting Star

- Bearish reversal pattern
- Has a wick at least half the candle length
- Shows that sellers have taken control and pushed the price down

Hanging Man

- Indicates an increase in selling pressure during an uptrend
- Looks like a hammer, but the wick continues briefly past the body
- Poses a threat to the downside

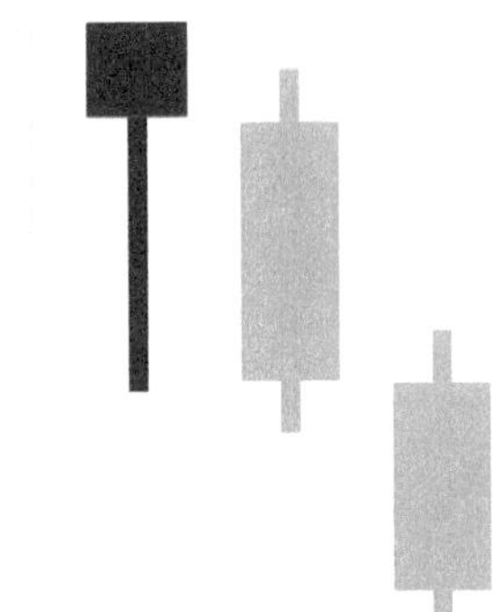

Gravestone Doji

- Formed when the open, low, and closing price share the same values, with a long upper shadow
- Occurs when buyers are able to push prices upwards, but resistance pushes it back to the open

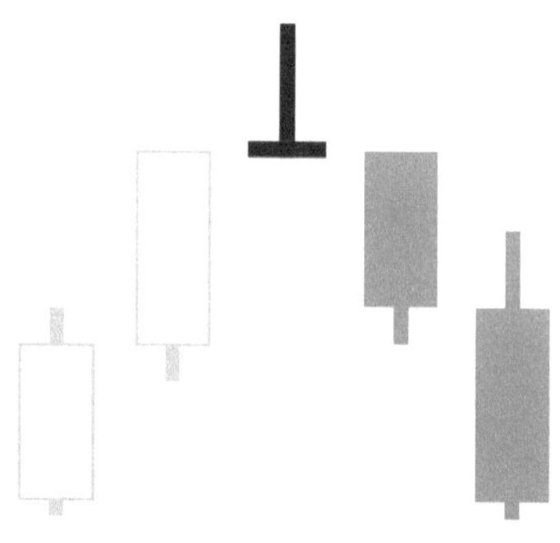

Bearish Engulfing

- Shows strong selling pressure
- Opens at or above the previous candle's
- close
- Body engulfs the previous candle and closes below its open

Dark Cloud Cover

- Bearish reversal pattern
- Piercing lines through candle after an uptrend
- Appears in an uptrend
- Signals potential weakness and that sellers could gain control

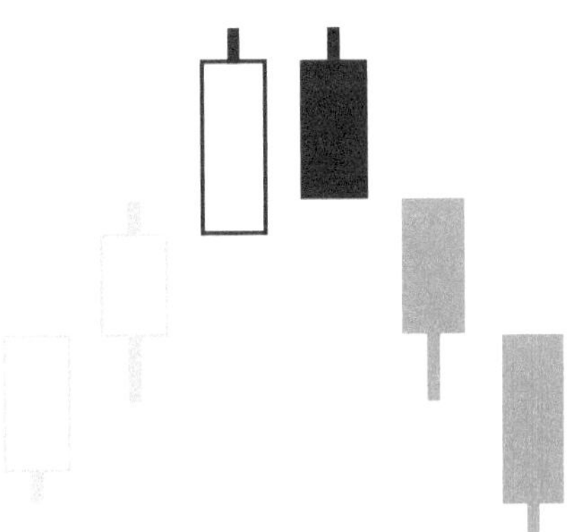

Evening Star

- Opposite of a morning star
- Reversal pattern found at the top of an uptrend
- A strong indicator is if the volume on the 3rd
- candle (the bearish candle) is greater than the volume on the first

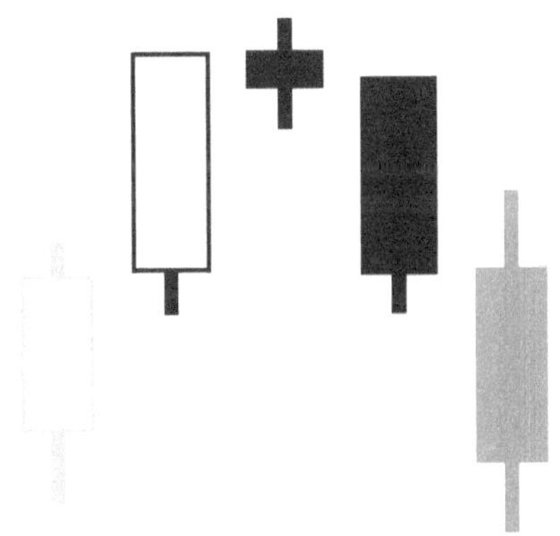

Doji

- Shows indecision between buyers and sellers
- Has the same open and close price
- If formed after a series of hollow candles, it could indicate that whoever is in control is losing strength

Spinning Top

- Similar to a doji
- Formation bearing another indecision
- Could be sign of a reversal if formed after a large move up or down

Do not anticipate and move without market confirmation – being a little late in your trade is your insurance that you are right or wrong

– Jesse Livermore

Chart Patterns

This section contains the chart patterns that I only focus on. They seem to be the most reliable patterns, and with everyone having access to the same charts, patterns, and information, they usually end up developing as people try to trade with the herd, not against.

These patterns are not fit to scale, nor will there usually ever be a perfect pattern all of the time, but the farther out the time frame is on the chart, the more reliable the pattern will be. This is why it is vital to have a good understanding of support & resistance and leverage. Some patterns that you will come across, you may not be able to give yourself a 3:1 profit/loss ratio. This could be a time of reflection and realizing that it might not be a good idea to place that trade.

Flags

Flags get their name from their appearance, and are a result of tight sideways price action amid a strong trend in the price. It can be constructed using two parallel trend lines that look like a flag when seen on the chart after a large spike in price. Volume generally declines during the flag formation, which is often followed by breakouts.

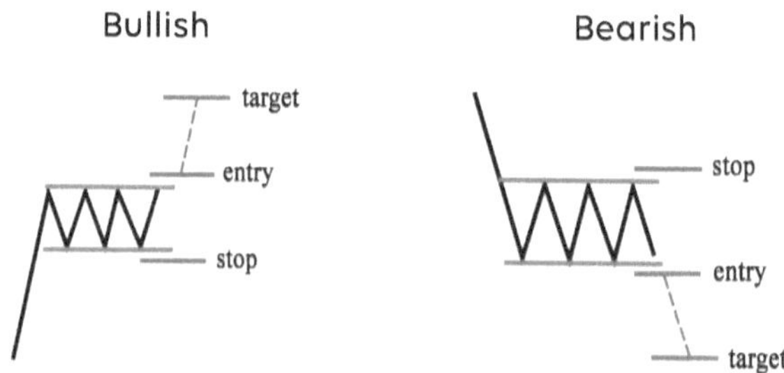

Pennants

A Pennant is a consolidation pattern formed by a sharp increase in price, thereby creating a flagpole shaped candle. It then has a period of consolidation that usually breaks out in the direction of the trend. Like flags, a Pennant is also accompanied by declining volumes.

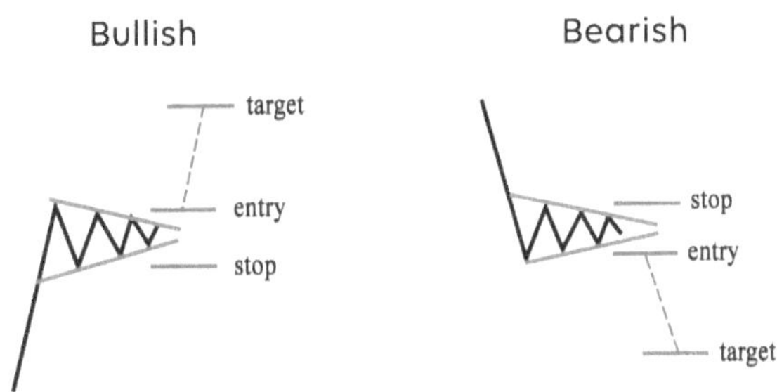

Rising and Falling Wedges

There are two types of wedges, rising and falling. A rising wedge signals a bearish reversal pattern and a falling wedge signals a bullish reversal could be forming. These shapes have been known to have a high probability.

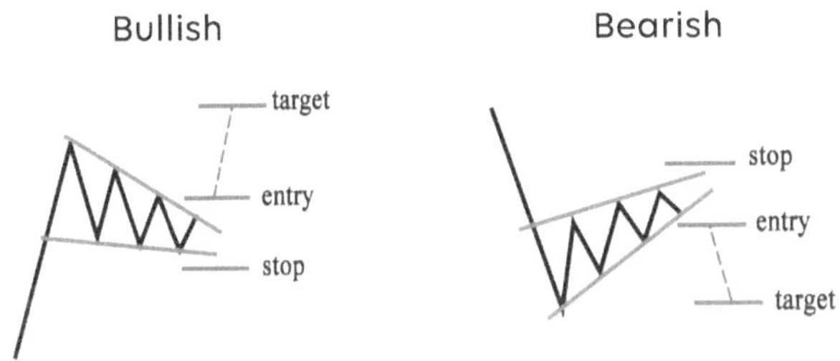

Cup and Handle

A cup and handle is a powerful pattern formed in an uptrend, signifying that the uptrend would resume once the formation is complete. The pattern looks like a cup on the left with a small handle on the side. An Inverse-Cup and handle would be identical to this, but upside down. The cup part of the pattern is a "U" shape pattern while the handle part is more of a wedge or pennant. Below is a chart demonstrating a cup and handle pattern.

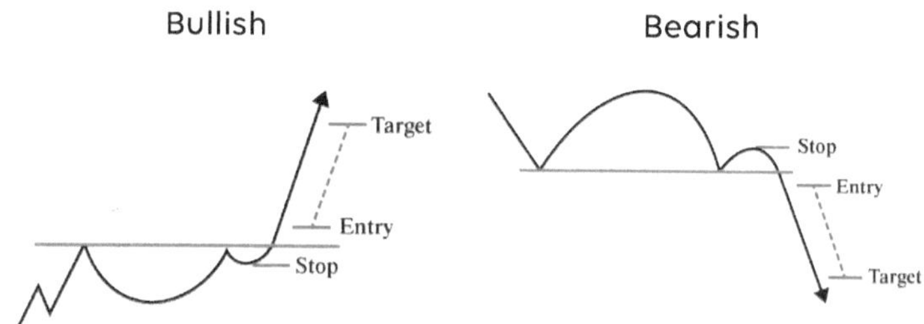

Triangles

Another pattern that has high probability is the Triangle. Triangles are prolonged consolidation patterns that result in either a breakdown or breakout depending on the kind of triangle formation. There are three types of triangle formations: symmetrical, ascending or descending.

Ascending   Descending

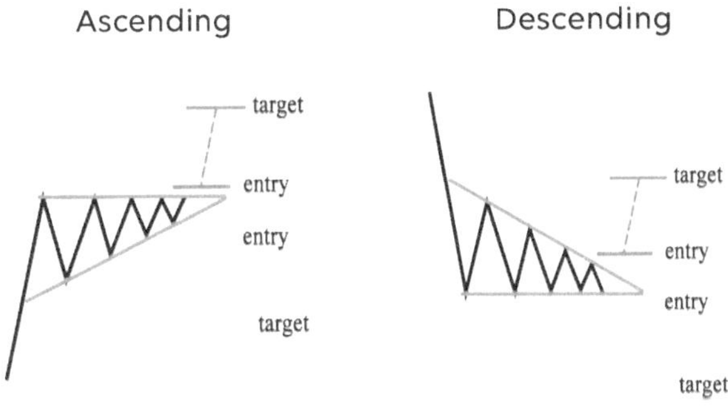

Symmetrical

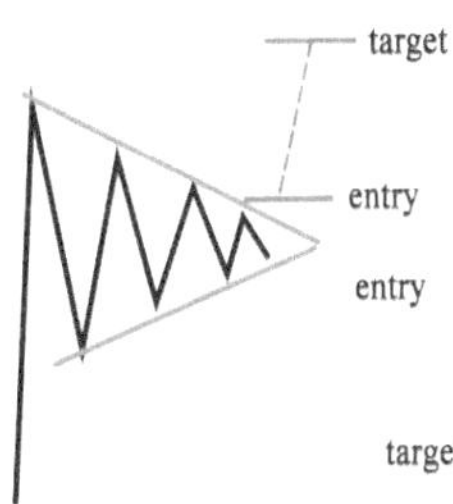

Head and Shoulders

Head and shoulders patterns appear at the end of any trend. This pattern resembles a head and shoulder, with the first shoulder formed in the direction of the trend followed by a price reversal. The price again comes back up and surpasses the earlier shoulder level and touches a new high/low, forming the head, before coming back again. The price again moves up/down, forming the second shoulder while coming back again, marking the reversal of the trend.

In a head and shoulder pattern, the price is not able to break new highs/lows after three attempts, signifying the reversal of the ongoing trend.

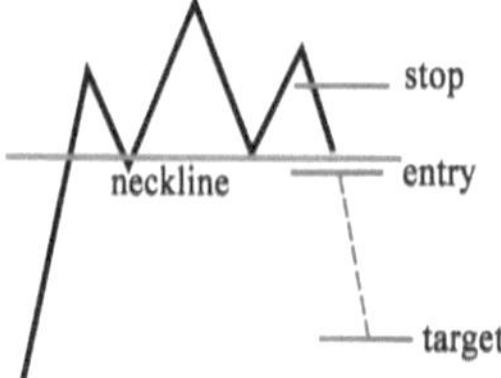

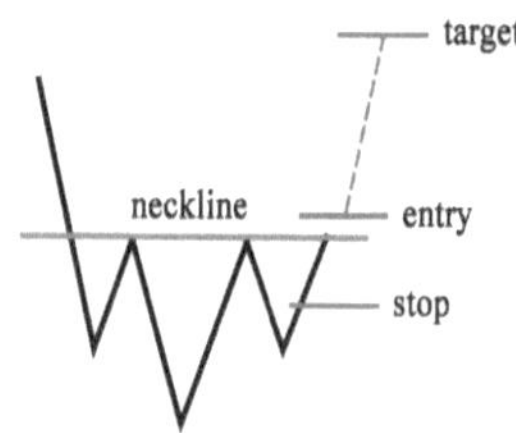

Double Top and Bottoms

Similar to head and shoulders patterns, double tops and bottoms are formed at the end of the uptrend and downtrend, respectively, signifying two failed attempts by the price to breach earlier highs/lows. Volatility increases during this pattern formation, indicating that the torchbearers of the trend (bulls or bears) are losing their breath.

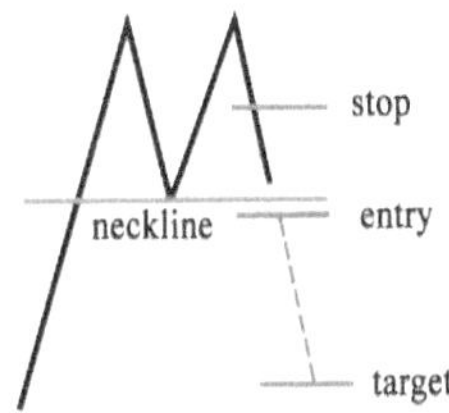

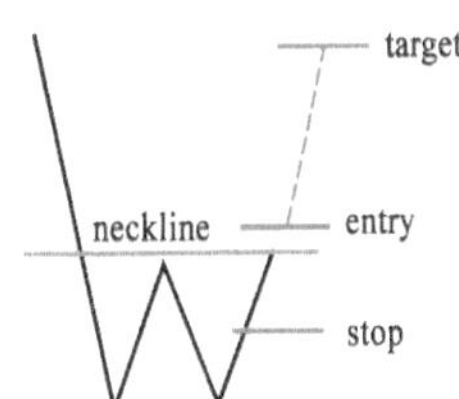

Triple Top and Bottom

One of the most powerful chart patterns is the triple top or bottom. This pattern signifies three futile attempts to reach a new high, often leading to reversals. In the event that it does break past the support or resistance level, it could very well reach new highs or lows

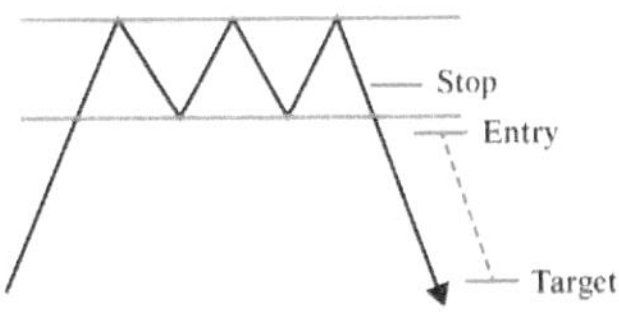

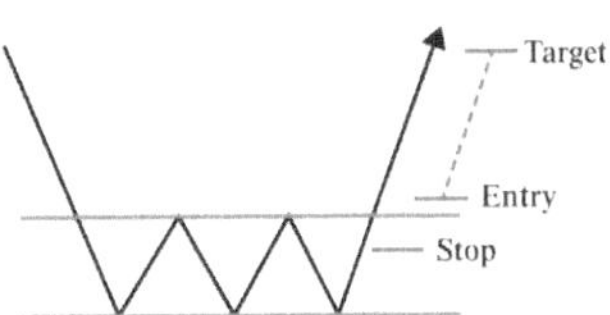

Summary

Like any other trading technique or strategy, price action trading also has its share of hits and misses. It requires an optimum level of risk taking and risk management. You will undoubtedly experience false breakouts, unidentifiable patterns, and many other negative surprises that will make your job as a trader difficult. While a losing trade cannot be avoided, the goal is to manage these effectively. Every trading strategy should have strong stop-loss rules. You won't be right all the time in this business; therefore, your mission is to set a plan and stick to it, otherwise you will incur losses.

It's not what happens to you, but how you react to
it that matters

- Epictetus

START

Moving Averages

Moving averages are as simple as they sound. In trading, a moving average is the average of the asset's closing price for a specified period. For example, a 10 day moving average is calculated as the average closing price for the last 10 trading days. These moving averages can then be plotted on a chart along with the price to obtain useful trading signals.

In the chart below, we use four Moving Averages. These are the 200 day, the 50 day, 20 day, and 9 day moving averages. As you can see, the farther out the time frame for the moving average, the less of a response you will see in the line.

Significance of Moving Averages

The importance of moving average can not be ignored in technical analysis. They are the simplest and one of the most powerful indicators. For starters, moving average tells you the following about the price of an asset:

I. **Trend of the Asset price**
II. **Strength of the Trend**
III. **The forward momentum and when the momentum is losing steam**
IV. **Support and Resistance levels**

Types of Moving Averages

Moving averages can either be simple or exponential. In a simple moving average, all prices in the average carry the same weight, meaning it moves somewhat slowly. In an exponential moving average, the more recent period prices carry a higher weight in the average, hence providing a recency to the average and making it more reflective of the current price move.

The rewards of keeping it simple are immense for traders, and those who understand it go a long way. So, let's discuss some of the major strategies that you can use to trade Forex using moving averages.

Moving Average Crossover

The most basic strategy one can use is to buy or sell when the moving averages cross. The simplicity of this strategy makes it hard to implement, since something this simple is not expected to make any profits. Contrary to this belief, this simple strategy has been extremely helpful in trading. As always, the longer time frame you use, the more reliable the chart will be. In the chart below, the 50-day moving average provided a nice trading opportunity when it broke through the 200 day moving average.

Such opportunities are extremely common in Forex trading, provided a trader uses them proactively with strict stop losses.

Using Moving Averages as Support and Resistance

Moving averages can also be used as support and resistance. Many traders use moving averages as psychological levels to place their trades. To do this successfully, you need to make sure you are trading in the overall direction of the trend.

In an uptrend, the prices see frequent intermittent corrections, which tend to reverse when they approach or reach moving average levels. In a downtrend, intermittent pull-ups are reversed at the moving average levels.

Moving averages are extremely customizable indicators that provide a trader with great trading signals. History has shown that, despite all the complex trading indicators available to a trader, moving averages are the simplest and most effective. With some practice and a good deal of risk management, traders can ace this indicator and trade profitably for long periods of time.

"I learned not to worry so much about the outcome but to concentrate on the step I was on and try to do it as perfectly as I could when I was doing it"

– Steve Wozniak

SOME HELPFUL TOOLS

In this section:

What Moves the Forex Market?

In general, market moves are determined by the supply and demand of that market's constituents. In foreign exchange (Forex) markets, these constituents are currencies of different countries. Changes in demand or supply of a currency leads to changes in the price of that currency. Supply and demand for currencies is impacted by many factors, but they can be grouped into two main categories: macroeconomic factors and geopolitical factors.

Macroeconomic Factors

Macroeconomics often dictates major movements in the Forex markets. An economy's overall strength is gauged by indicators such as economic growth, inflation, employment and wage levels, interest rate movements, central bank actions, and trade and capital flows. These are widely tracked, high frequency indicators released by authorities on specified dates. Each of these macroeconomic factors impacts the markets in unique ways.

Economic Growth, Inflation, and other High Frequency Data

Market experts and economists forecast and estimate these data points before they are officially published. Because traders price currencies based on those forecasts, surprise discrepancies between the forecasts and actual data often result in significant market movements, both positive and negative. A positive surprise leads to higher demand for the local currency due to capital influx. This increased demand then pushes the local currency prices higher in comparison to other currencies. Conversely, a negative surprise does just the opposite and pulls prices down. Currencies also respond to economic policies. For example, a forthcoming capitalist economy may experience a rise in the price of its currency as compared to others, while a closed, opaque economy may experience a declining value, assuming all other factors remain the same. Forex traders track economic data closely and keep a calendar to plan their trades around the release of this data.

Interest Rate Movements

According to basic economic principles, higher interest rates attract more capital to an economy. As a forex trader, this means that you should be on the lookout for signs of growth and inflation. This will ultimately determine the direction of an economy's interest rates. Large amounts of money will flow to countries with high interest rates, pushing the value of its currency higher compared to other currencies.

Central Bank Actions

Central Banks also intervene in the Forex markets through both direct and indirect measures. An example of a direct measure is buying and selling currencies to counter excess volatility. Indirect measures include loosening capital flow restrictions or releasing liquidity into the markets.

External Trade and Balance of Payments

A currency's demand also depends on its trade balance with the external world. If the country is a net exporter, it will typically have a strengthening currency (assuming everything else remains the same). This is because traders will buy the country's currency to pay for their merchandise, leading to increased demand and a higher value.

A country's currency will also experience high demand if it is a popular investment destination that attracts significant short-term and long-term capital flows. Countries with high trade deficits can also experience rising currencies if they attract large capital flows.

Flight to Safety

When economies face extraordinarily turbulent times, investors and traders often move their capital to safer countries like the United States and other developed countries. This weakening of riskier, vulnerable currencies such as the AUD and NZD leads traders to flock to safe-haven currencies such as the CHF, JPY, and USD. This usually causes the unwinding of many carry trades and can lead to significant price movements.

Geopolitical Factors

While major Forex movements can happen due to macroeconomic factors, geopolitics also contributes its share of influence. Countries marred by political uncertainties will often have dwindling currencies that can lose much of their value as traders lose confidence in the currency. This can also happen to countries on the brink of war or fighting insurgencies and dictatorships.

Natural Disasters

Natural disasters represent a black swan event for many people. They can happen at any time and are extremely difficult to prepare for, even for stable, developed countries. Commodity prices tend to see huge swings when disasters occur, so keep an eye on countries that are large exporters of goods and have been affected by a tragedy.

Conclusion

Most Forex traders spend a good share of their time analyzing macro data and trading according to their individual strategies. Some smart traders only look for extraordinary events (like Brexit or the financial crisis) to find prime opportunities to trade Forex. Forex market movements can be better understood by observing the macro data and reactions by market participants after the release of economic data. A detailed analysis of historical data can provide useful insights when developing a strategy. The Forex market is extremely dynamic, and traders must constantly remain on their toes to respond not only to the discussed factors, but also to a host of other factors. Learning to deal with uncertainty is of utmost importance if you want to be a successful Forex trader.

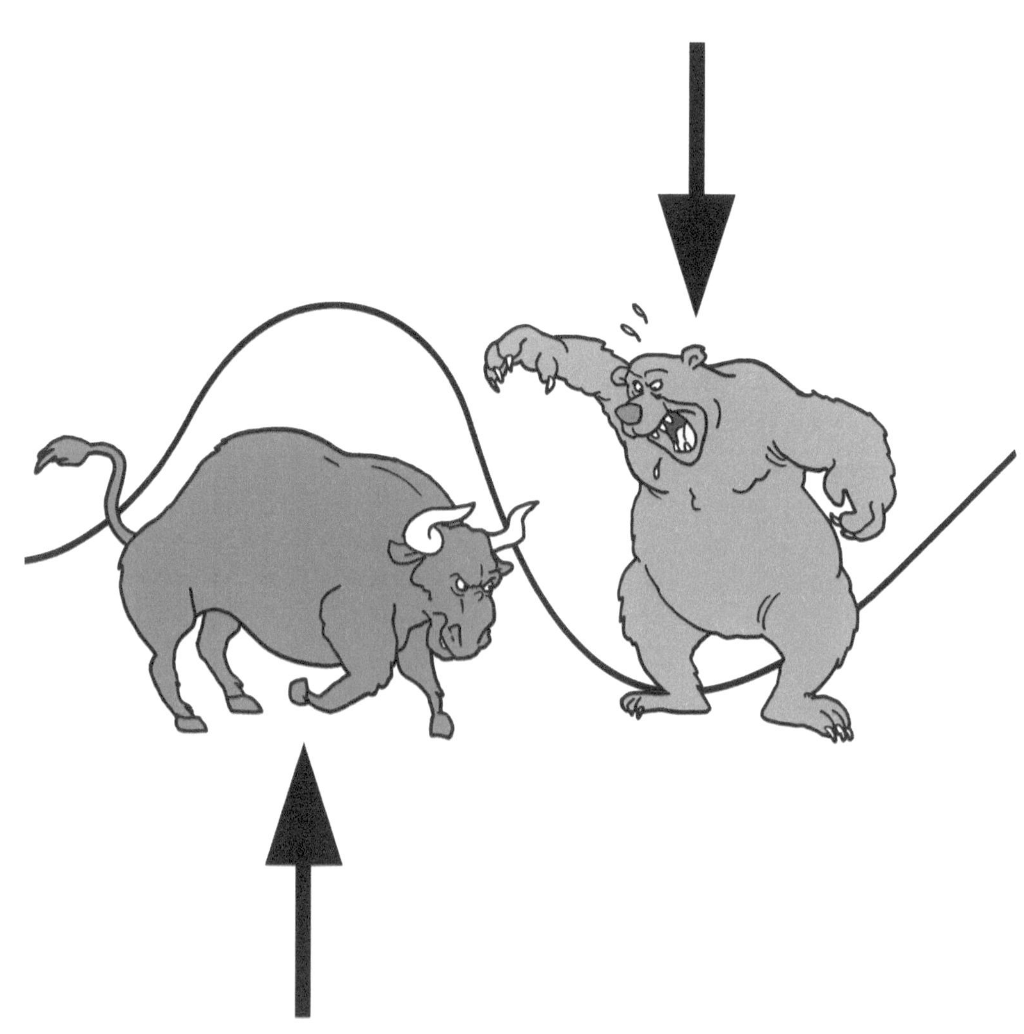

Support & Resistance

Support and resistance are two important concepts that form the basis of many traders' core strategy. Support is the level at which price stops falling and stabilizes, eventually reversing into an uptrend. Resistance is the level at which price stops rising, stabilizes, and reverts to the downtrend. Support and resistance are levels from which the price of currencies, or any other asset, tends to retrace back forth within a minor or major trend.

The Basic Psychology

Support and resistance are basically zones of supply and demand. Whenever the price of a currency is declining within a larger uptrend and reaches a support level, it sees an impending demand from traders pushing the price back up, resuming the uptrend. Similarly, whenever an up-trending currency reaches its resistance level, it meets a lack of demand, pushing the price back down.

Putting Support and Resistance in Context

Support and resistance must be understood in the overall context of the trend. Generally, prices can be viewed as being within both a long-term and short-term trend. The charts you choose to use are dependent on the trade you are doing. For instance, you may choose the daily chart as your long-term trend if you are trading on an hourly chart or you may choose the hourly chart as your long-term trend if you are trading on a five-minute chart.

Price can be trending up in the long-term trend and trending down in the short-term trend at the same time. Typically when that happens, the short-term trend reverses at the support zone and moves into the direction of the long-term trend.

Similarly, in a long-term downtrend the price can be moving up in the short-term trend. The price reverses downward once it hits the resistance level.

Identifying Support and Resistance

Support and resistance can be determined by studying the previous price behavior. If the price tends to retract, or bounce back, from a particular price level two or more times, that level can be termed as support or resistance.

In the chart above, the price hits the support (lower line) and resistance (upper line) level multiple times before finally breaking the support and heading down. Once the price is in new territory, though, establishing new support and resistance levels becomes difficult because using the earlier price history - which was far into the past – is less relevant.

In such cases, traders use trendlines or moving averages as support and resistance levels. These trend lines are drawn by connecting lows of the current uptrend as shown in Figure 2. Once the price hits two or more intermittent lows and bounces back from those lows, one can connect these lows and form a trendline. Price would normally find support along a diagonal line upwards. In this case, the price moved back up after coming near the trend line multiple times before finally breaking through the trendline, shifting into a downtrend.

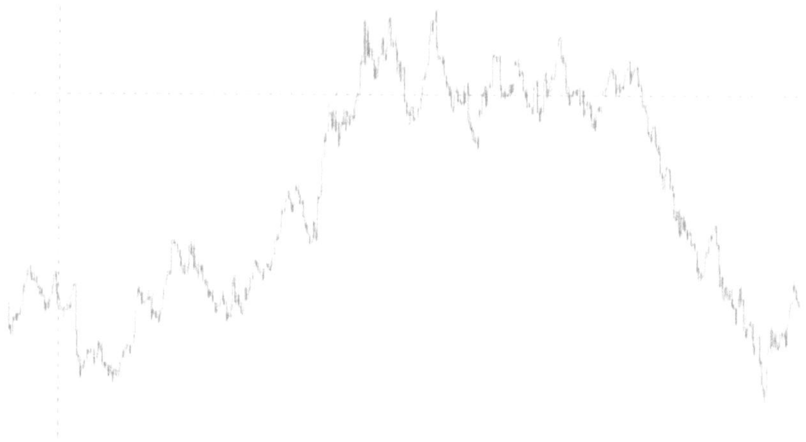

Similarly, a trendline can be drawn by connecting 2 or more price highs, demonstrating price resistance. It is helpful to trade in a downtrend. When the price is in a downtrend and bounces back up for a brief period, it moves towards the downward sloping trendline. After hitting the trendline, the price reverses back into the downtrend, creating a resistance zone.

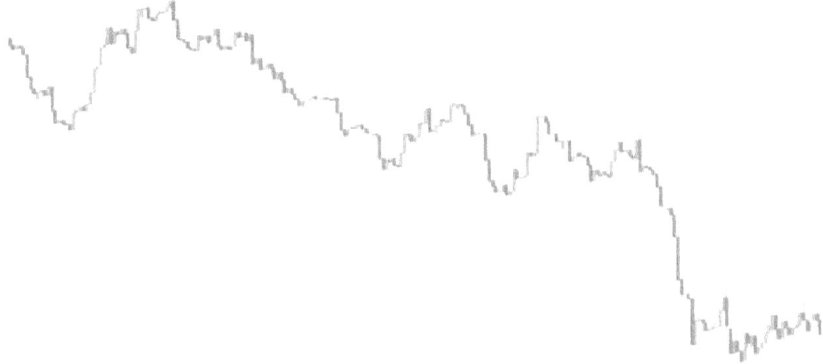

One can also identify support and resistance using moving averages. Unlike trendlines, moving averages don't have to be drawn and are automatically laid out by your charting software once you specify the interval. A moving average is simply the average of prices over the past period specified by the user. For example, if you lay out a 50-day moving average on a daily chart, you will get a smoothed line, plotting the average price during the preceding 50 days.

In the picture below, price hits the 50-day moving average line multiple times, essentially acting as support while price moves upward.

Major and Minor Support and Resistance

Minor supports and resistances are interim levels at which the price is expected to reverse. Major support and resistance levels to be the levels where the price has seen major trend reversals. Major supports and resistances are considered to be hard to break.

Entry, Exit, and Stop Losses

While trading on support and resistance, your entry point will most likely be at support for a long position and at resistance in the case of a short position. Most traders wait for a confirmation of the price retracement before entering into a position.

Exits typically happen when the price touches the opposite price level. This means that in a long position, traders exit when price touches resistance and in a short position, exits happen when the price touches support levels.

Stop losses are mostly placed a few points below the support for long positions and a few points above resistance for short positions.

False Breakouts and Breakdowns

Price does not always stop at support and resistance zones. Sometimes price extends its decline or advance. When this happens, traders may conclude that a trend reversal has happened and the support and resistance levels no longer hold. However, in most instances the price does come back after a brief penetration, once more moving in the direction of the broader trend.

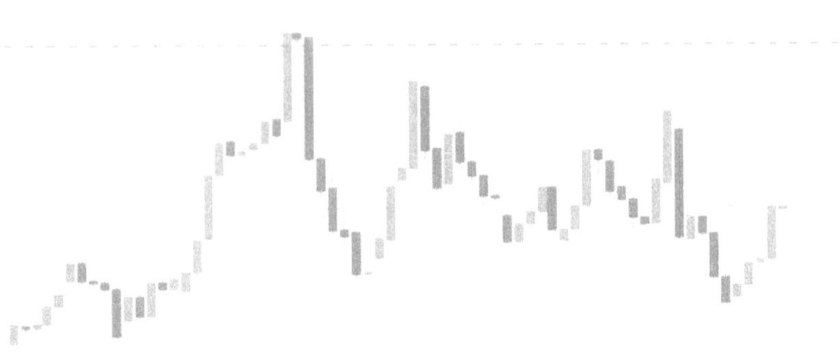

False breakouts and breakdowns are excellent trading opportunities and traders should be on the lookout for them. The correct entry point after a false breakout or breakdown would be when the price comes back through the support or resistance level.

Conclusion

Support and resistance are easy and powerful trading tools that should be in the arsenal of every trader. It takes a lot of practice to master these techniques and make consistent profits out of any trading strategy you follow. As a trader, you would do best to practice your trading technique with good risk management, keeping a tight hold on your losses by using stop losses diligently.

Whenever I enter a position, I have a predetermined stop. That is the only way I can sleep. I know where I'm getting out before I get in. The position size on a trade is determined by the stop, and the stop is determined on a technical basis

- Bruce Kovner

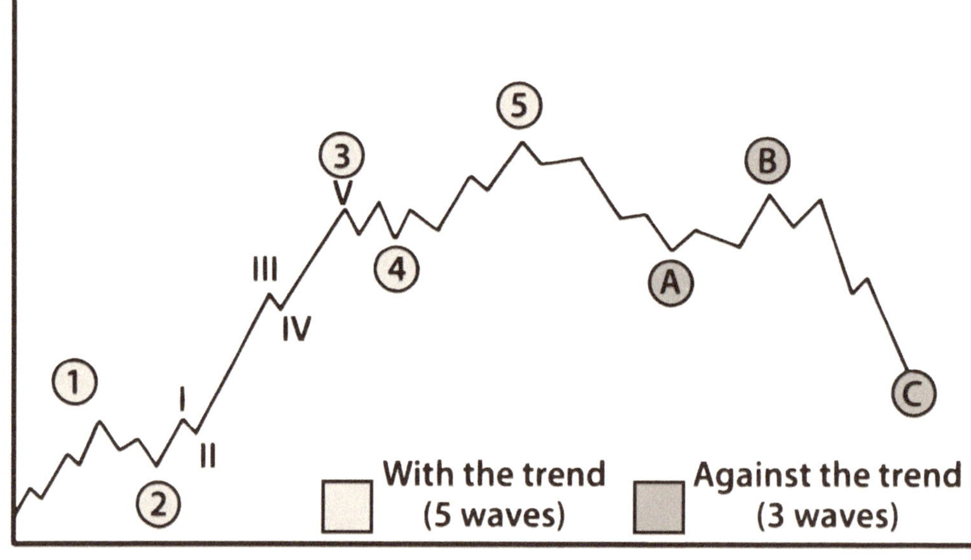

①
②
I
II
III
IV
3
V
4
5
A
B
C
With the trend
(5 waves)
Against the trend
(3 waves)

Elliott Wave Theory

Developed by Ralph Nelson Elliott in the 1930s and popularized by Robert Prechter in the 1970s, Elliott Wave Theory emphasizes that markets consistently demonstrate the same types of long-term and short-term patterns, which Elliot described as fractal wave patterns. According to Elliot, such patterns not only apply to financial markets, but also to other situations in which many people come together and act simultaneously. Examples of this include situations like buying homes or taking out loans.

A Brief History

Elliot posited his theory after meticulously studying index movements dating back 75 years. His detailed study included analyzing yearly, monthly, weekly, daily, and self-made hourly and 30-minute charts.

After studying the data, Elliot specified rules on identifying, predicting, and capitalizing on the wave patterns formed by the markets. He also noted that these patterns cannot predict exact future price movements, but they can be helpful in figuring out future market corrections. These patterns, when used alongside other indicators, can provide useful insights on the current state of the market. As such, they can also help you cash in on specific opportunities.

All of Elliot's work is covered in "R.N. Elliott's Masterworks," published in 1994.

The Theory

The theory states that crowd psychology works in certain patterns, which repeat themselves over time. Financial markets follow these patterns because markets bring together large flocks of people with differing views on trading.

The theory also states that the price movements are predictable because they tend to follow the same repeating wave pattern. These waves are called *motive* waves and *corrective* waves. Together, they form the Elliott Wave pattern.

Motive Wave – The First Half of Elliott Wave Theory

A motive wave is a wave that always advances in the direction of the trend of one larger degree. For instance, there will be many smaller types of waves and patterns in a 5 minute chart which are not so reliable, that build and form the overall weekly and daily charts.

As shown in the following picture, the wave is further subdivided into five smaller sub-waves, three of which – 1, 3 and 5 – move in the direction of the larger trend (up) and are called actionary sub-waves. The other two – 2 and 4 – move in the direction opposite to the larger trend (down) and are called corrective sub-waves. The following picture depicts the application of the theory when the larger trend is an uptrend. Its application remains the same when the larger trend is a downtrend.

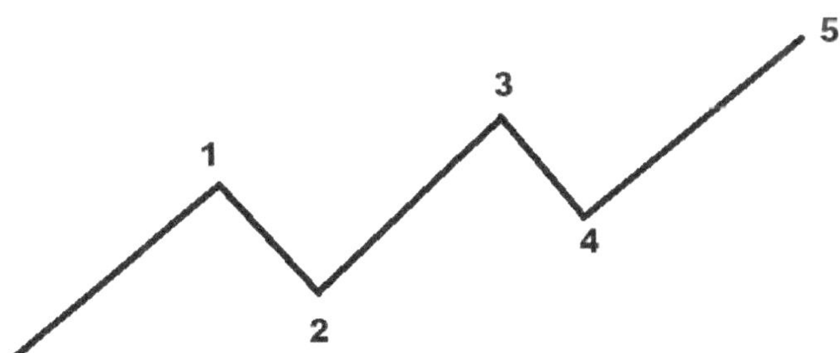

There are three rules that must be satisfied when considering motive wave formation:
1. Wave 2 always retracts less than 100% of Wave 1.
2. Wave 3 always goes past wave 1 and is longer most of the time.
3. Wave 4 retracts less than wave 3, leading to the final wave 5 to complete the pattern

Corrective Wave - The Second Half of Elliott Wave Theory

A corrective wave is a three sub-wave pattern, as shown in the chart below. It forms after the motive wave and depicts the correction within the larger trend.

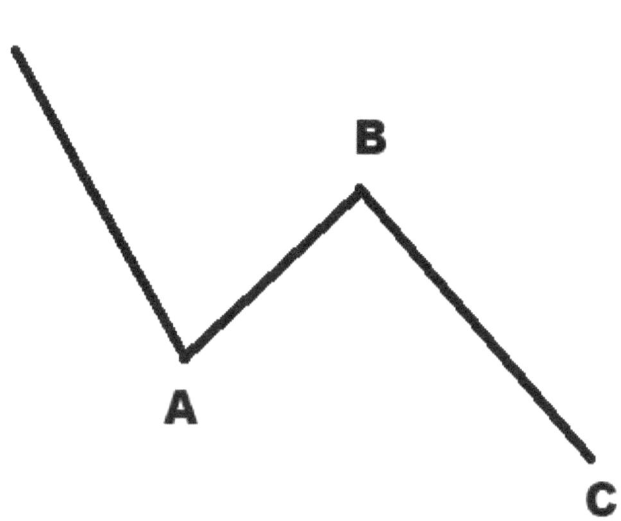

A corrective wave pattern is laid out as a three-wave structure. Wave A is the reverse of the main overall trend, where sellers are gaining traction. Wave B is formed when buyers come back into play but just can't seem to gain control, wherein wave C is formed when sellers completely gain control. This can lead to a deeper sell off or it may start the full wave all over again.

Remember

Per the theory, this structure is repeated again and again, forming a 5-3-5-3-5 structure. These are very good points that you should become very familiar with, as these will be what you are looking to trade. You want to make sure you ride the wave in the right direction.

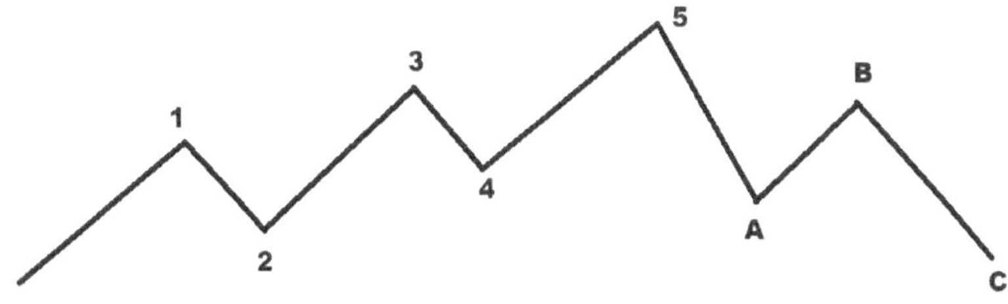

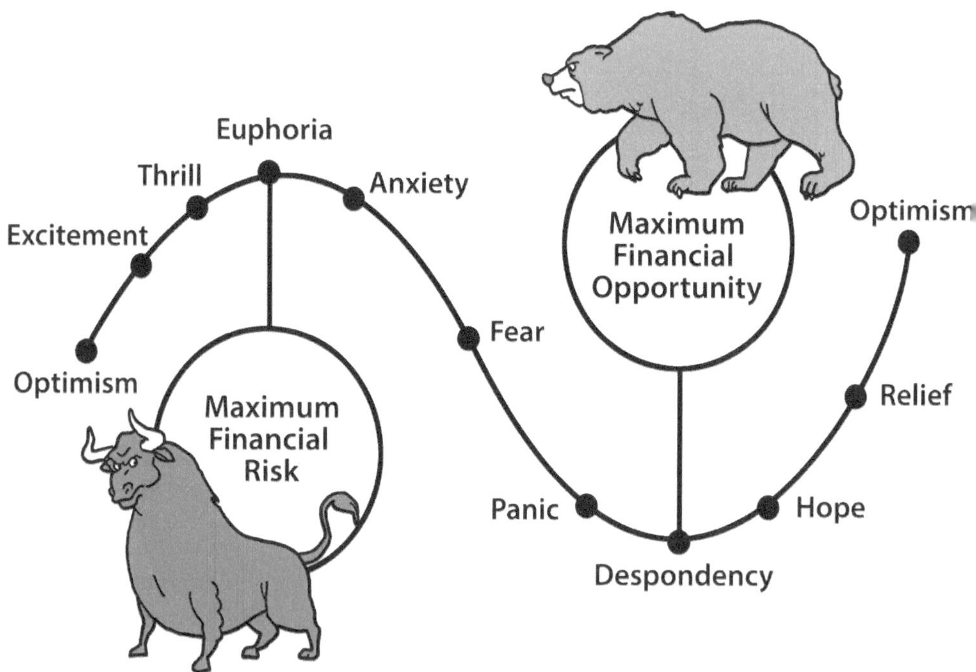

Euphoria
Thrill
Anxiety
Excitement
Optimism
Maximum Financial Risk
Fear
Maximum Financial Opportunity
Optimism
Relief
Panic
Hope
Despondency

Understanding Market Sentiment

Market sentiment is how traders feel towards a particular currency pair or towards the entire market at a particular point in time. The gauge is an additional tool in the trader's arsenal to improve her odds at trading.

The market sentiment reveals the psychology of traders towards the market. The sentiment can range from extreme pessimism to extreme optimism.

Generally, rising prices are tied to positive market sentiment while falling prices signify negative market sentiment. A trader can use complex tools, indicators, and data sources to understand the mood of the market to make adequately informed trading decisions.

Market Sentiment Analysis in Forex Trading

Sentiment analysis in forex trading gives the trader a clearer indication of where the market is headed. One of the most prominent ways to gauge market sentiment is by looking at the long-short ratio. If the ratio is tilted toward longs, it signifies a bullish sentiment and if the tilt is toward shorts, it signifies a bearish sentiment. For example, if the long-short ratio is 4:1, it means that 80% of traders are long while 20% are short, which is a highly bullish sentiment.

The following are a couple of important indicators and data sources forex traders can use to understand the market sentiment in forex markets.

Moving Averages

Moving Averages are the simplest indicators forex traders can use to ascertain market sentiment. One can use short-term (21 periods), medium-term (50 periods) and long-term (200 periods) moving averages to check for short, medium, and long-term sentiment, respectively.

If the price of a currency pair is trading above its moving average, it is said to be in an uptrend (bullish sentiment). The opposite is true for a downtrend (bearish sentiment). Change in sentiment happens when the price crosses the moving average line. For example, if the price moves from below the moving average line to above, the trend is considered to be changed from downtrend to uptrend and the sentiment from bearish to bullish.

In the chart below, the price broke through all of the moving averages from above, but dipped only temporarily below the 200-day moving average, beginning a strong uptrend.

Commitment of Traders Report

The Commitment of Traders report is a weekly report published by the Commodity Futures Trading Commission (CFTC), and is prepared using submissions of large traders in the futures market. The report shows the long and short positions, along with the net open interest in a currency.

The report is further segmented into positions by commercial and non-commercial traders. Commercial traders are organizations that have a business interest behind their positions while non-commercial traders are large speculators and traders like hedge funds.

The report gives strong sentiment cues for major currencies such as: USD, JPY, GBP, and EUR. Large short open-interest in a currency depicts negative sentiment, while large long open-interest depicts positive sentiment.

The Final Word

There is a saying amongst traders: "The trend is your friend." A successful trend-trader makes huge amounts of money by just identifying the trend and trading in the direction of the trend. Knowing the market sentiment helps the trader confirm the market trend, making their life easier.

The market sentiment indicators can also offer cues of upcoming turning points. For example, when volume is weak, yet the change in open interest is quite high in the direction opposite the current trend, that may be an indication that the trend is getting exhausted and a reversal may be just around the corner.

A majority of your money will be made following the trend; conversely, the majority of your losses will occur during reversals. Therefore, market sentiment can be useful to stay ahead of the curve. Your objective is to trade the trend and exit before reversals. A good trader will check the market sentiment indicators periodically to remain objective while trading, instead of getting carried away by price movements.

Play the market only when all factors are in your favor. No person can play the market all the time and win. There are times when you should be completely out of the market, for emotional as well as economic reasons

- Jesse Livermore

Conclusion

I want to leave you with a story. There is a brief chapter in Homer's poem, The Odyssey, about Odysseus and the Island of the Sirens.

In ancient Greece, there was a legendary hero named Odysseus who lived off the coast of Athens. He was set to sail on a treacherous journey, but before doing so he met with a sorceress, named Circe, who warned him of what he would encounter on his trip. She warned him of the Sirens, who were dangerous vultures. From a distance, though, they gave the illusion of being beautiful women with voices of angels.

Their singing was known to be so beautiful that it would cause sailors to throw themselves off their ships and into the rocks, in search of the woman. This is when the sly Sirens would attack and feed on the sailors.

Circe had also told him that if one heard the singing of the Sirens and survived, that person would become wiser.

So Odysseus, being the brave warrior that he was, set off on the journey with his crew members, seeking to hear the beautiful sounds of the Sirens. As they approached the island, Odysseus had his crew tie him to the mast of the ship so he could not move. This would stop him from jumping ship. And the sailors? He had them stuff their ears with wax to prevent them from hearing the songs that would erase their *willpower*.

As they approached the island, the mesmerizing sounds of the Sirens tugged at Odysseus's soul. But he could not break free. He yelled and screamed to have the sailors set him free, but they would not. They stuck to the plan and the sailors survived.

Now, keep this story in mind during your trading. Distractions such as news and social media can throw off your trading success. Our secret to success has always been to keep things simple and stick to the plan.

www.ingramcontent.com/pod-product-compliance
Lightning Source LLC
Chambersburg PA
CBHW021123130726
47988CB00003B/1133